NEW JERSEY

NEW JERSEY

HELLO
U.S.A.

by Charles Fredeen

Lerner Publications Company

You'll find this picture of flowers in a greenhouse at the beginning of every chapter. New Jersey is known as the Garden State because of the many flowers, vegetables, fruits, shrubs, and trees grown there. Although New Jersey is one of the most crowded states in the country, New Jerseyans still find space to plant flower and vegetable gardens, maintain orchards, and run farms.

Cover (left): Sunset on Barnegat Bay, Long Beach Island. Cover (right): A fairground on a boardwalk, New Jersey. Pages 2–3: Horses pull a stagecoach at the World Pair Driving Championships, Gladstone. Page 3: Horseshoe crabs, Cape May.

Copyright © 2002 by Lerner Publications Company

This book is available in two editions:
Library binding by Lerner Publications Company, a division of Lerner Publishing Group
Soft cover by First Avenue Editions, an imprint of Lerner Publishing Group
241 First Avenue North
Minneapolis, MN 55401 U.S.A.

Website address: www.lernerbooks.com

LIBRARY OF CONGRESS CATALOGING-IN-PUBLICATION DATA

Fredeen, Charles, 1956–
    New Jersey / by Charles Fredeen (Rev. and expanded 2nd ed.)
        p. cm. — (Hello U.S.A.)
    Includes index.
    ISBN 0-8225-4060-6 (lib. bdg.: alk. paper)
    ISBN 0-8225-4148-3 (pbk.: alk. paper)
    1. New Jersey—Juvenile literature. [1. New Jersey] I. Title. II. Series.
    F134.3 2002
    974.9—dc21   2001001164

Manufactured in the United States of America
1 2 3 4 5 6 – JR – 07 06 05 04 03 02

CONTENTS

The Seaside State

illions of years ago, dinosaurs lumbered across northern New Jersey, leaving their footprints in the mud. Only fossils and skeletons remind us that these giant, three-toed animals once lived in New Jersey—a state that millions of people call home.

Visitors to New Jersey can find more than 20 scenic lighthouses along the coast.

7

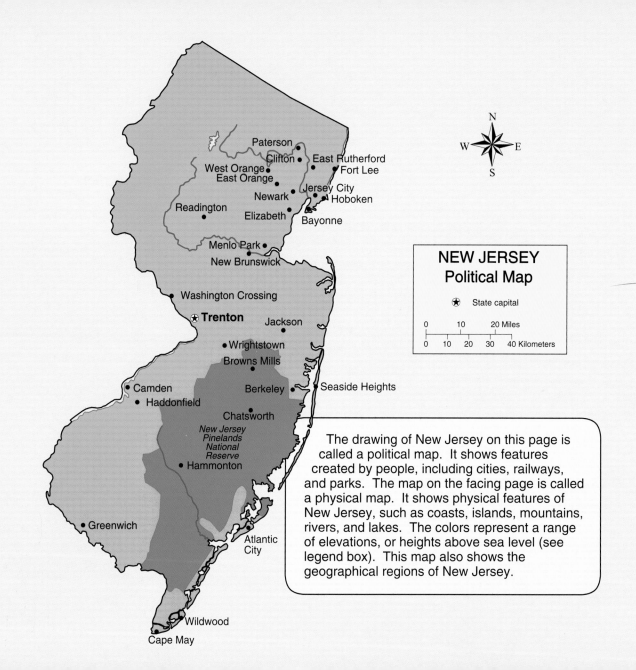

Paterson
Clifton
East Rutherford
Fort Lee
West Orange
East Orange
Newark
Jersey City
Hoboken
Readington
Elizabeth
Bayonne
Menlo Park
New Brunswick
Washington Crossing
⭐ **Trenton**
Jackson
• Wrightstown
Browns Mills
• Camden
Berkeley
Seaside Heights
• Haddonfield
Chatsworth
*New Jersey
Pinelands
National
Reserve*
• Hammonton
• Greenwich
Atlantic
City
Wildwood
Cape May

N
W   E
S

NEW JERSEY
Political Map

⭐ State capital

0	10		20 Miles
0	10	20	30	40 Kilometers

The drawing of New Jersey on this page is called a political map. It shows features created by people, including cities, railways, and parks. The map on the facing page is called a physical map. It shows physical features of New Jersey, such as coasts, islands, mountains, rivers, and lakes. The colors represent a range of elevations, or heights above sea level (see legend box). This map also shows the geographical regions of New Jersey.

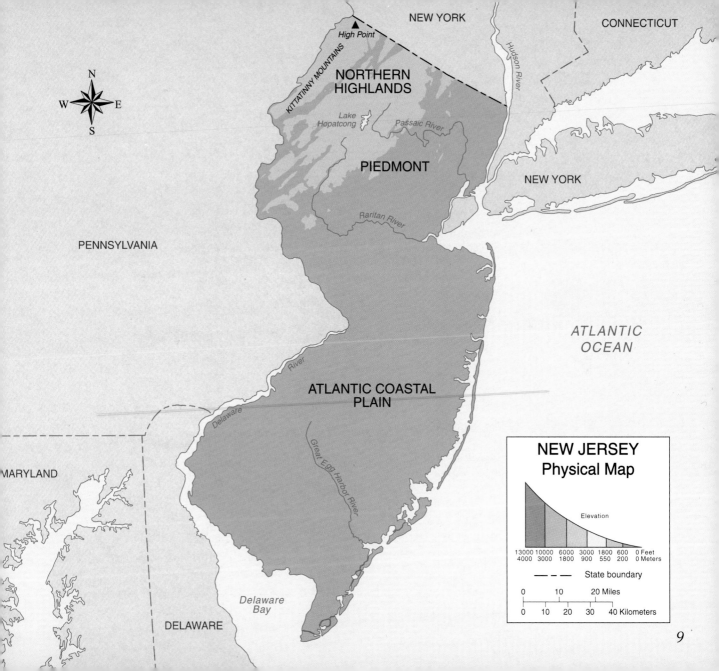

NEW YORK

CONNECTICUT

High Point

KITTATINNY MOUNTAINS

NORTHERN
HIGHLANDS

Lake
Hopatcong

Passaic River

Hudson River

PIEDMONT

NEW YORK

Raritan River

N
W E
S

PENNSYLVANIA

ATLANTIC
OCEAN

River

ATLANTIC COASTAL
PLAIN

Delaware

MARYLAND

Great Egg Harbor River

Delaware
Bay

DELAWARE

NEW JERSEY
Physical Map

Elevation

| 13000 | 10000 | 6000 | 3000 | 1800 | 600 | 0 Feet |
| 4000 | 3000 | 1800 | 900 | 550 | 200 | 0 Meters |

- - - State boundary

0   10   20 Miles

0   10   20   30   40 Kilometers

9

The Atlantic coastline stretches 130 miles along New Jersey's eastern border.

Lying along the Atlantic Ocean, New Jersey is a Middle Atlantic state. Water defines all but one of the state's boundaries. The Hudson River and the Atlantic Ocean form New Jersey's eastern border. Across the Delaware Bay, which is off New Jersey's southern coast, lies the state of Delaware. To the west, across the Delaware River, is Pennsylvania. To the north and east is New York.

Three land regions cut across New Jersey. Two small regions—the Northern Highlands and the Piedmont—cover northwestern New Jersey. The Atlantic Coastal Plain, the state's largest region, extends over the rest of the state.

High Point, the state's highest spot, rises in the Northern Highlands region. The peak is part of the Kittatinny Mountains, which are located in the northwestern corner of this region. The Kittatinnies are part of a large chain of mountains called the Appalachians. This long mountain chain runs from Canada to Alabama. Formed more than 200 million years ago, the Appalachians are the oldest mountains in North America.

In fall the changing leaves brighten the highlands of northern New Jersey.

Rivers have carved deep valleys between these mountains and between the smaller peaks of the Northern Highlands. Some of the mountains are rich in minerals such as iron and zinc. South of the Kittatinnies is Lake Hopatcong, the largest of New Jersey's 800 lakes.

Southeast of the Northern Highlands lies the gently rolling Piedmont, a region covered by a

On the Passaic River, a rainbow forms in the mist above a waterfall.

plateau, or broad expanse of high land. Most of the rivers in the region form waterfalls when they drop from the Piedmont to the lower, softer soil of the Atlantic Coastal Plain. An imaginary line called the **Fall Line** connects these waterfalls. Early pioneers settled along the Fall Line because their boats couldn't travel upstream past the falls. Over time, the settlements grew into some of New Jersey's biggest cities.

The Atlantic Coastal Plain slopes gently eastward from the Fall Line to

Families enjoy playing in the waves of the Atlantic Ocean.

the Atlantic Ocean. Millions of tourists vacation on New Jersey's ocean beaches every year. People also come to the southern part of the region to hike in the Pinelands—an area of winding rivers and forests of dwarf pine and miniature oak trees.

Many rivers cross New Jersey, but the two most important are the Hudson and the Delaware, both of which empty into the Atlantic Ocean. Ships bringing goods from all over the world dock at harbors along both rivers. Like many other rivers in New Jersey, the Passaic, Raritan, and Great Egg Harbor Rivers also flow into the Atlantic Ocean.

In northern New Jersey, a red farmhouse stands out against the snow. More snow falls in this part of the state than in southern New Jersey.

Ocean breezes cool sunbathers on New Jersey's seaside beaches in the summer. The average summertime temperature in New Jersey is 75° F, although it is cooler in the mountains of the northwestern part of the state. New Jersey's average winter temperature is 31° F. Winters are coldest in the mountains, where about 50 inches of snow fall each year. **Precipitation** (rain, snow, sleet, and hail) averages about 45 inches in the state each year.

Rain helps plants such as honeysuckle, mountain laurels, buttercups, and Queen Anne's lace grow in many parts of the state. The purple violet—New Jersey's state flower—is found in wooded areas.

Forests cover about 42 percent of New Jersey. Maple, birch, and yellow poplar trees grow in the northern part of the state, while cedars and pines thrive in the south. Deer, foxes, skunks, and mink roam the woods. Lurking in parts of northern New Jersey are two poisonous snakes—the rattlesnake and the copperhead.

Azaleas bloom in the spring in New Jersey.

New Jersey's coast is home to wading birds such as the blue heron *(above)* and shorebirds such as the piping plover *(above right)*.

Many types of birds and fish make their homes in and along New Jersey's rivers and coastal waters. Blue herons, ducks, and geese live in the marshy areas near the ocean. Clams, crabs, oysters, and lobsters live in the waters along the coast. And fishers are sure to find plenty of bass, pike, and trout in the state's many bays and streams.

THE HISTORY

Natives and Newcomers

cientists believe that people first came to North America more than 15,000 years ago by crossing a land bridge that once connected Asia to the North American continent. These people and their descendants are called Indians, or Native Americans. About 12,000 years ago, Indians made their way to what became New Jersey, where they hunted deer, caribou, and mastodons—giant hairy elephants with big tusks and huge teeth.

The First Roads in New Jersey

NEW YORK

PENNSYLVANIA

Delaware River

DELAWARE

ATLANTIC OCEAN

Thousands of years before Europeans settled in the New World, Lenape Indians lived on the land that became New Jersey. Some of the state's modern highways follow the trails blazed by these Indians.

Indian Trails
Minisink
Allamatunk
Old Cape Road
Burlington
Manahawkin
Cohansey

By 1500 B.C., many different groups of Indians had settled along North America's Atlantic coast. Those who lived in New Jersey are called Lenape, a word meaning "people of the same nation" or "ordinary people."

The Lenape lived in small villages. Several related families usually shared a longhouse—a low, long shelter made from wooden posts covered with bark or grasses. Each family had its own space in the longhouse for cooking, eating, and sleeping. The Lenape also built smaller bark shelters called wigwams, which housed only one family.

The Lenape used branches to build frames for shelters called longhouses. They covered the frames with bark or grasses.

Palm Trees in New Jersey?

Early drawings of Lenape Indians by Europeans were not always very accurate. For example, the Lenape didn't live in tepees *(background)*, nor did they wear feathered headdresses. Palm trees didn't grow in New Jersey, either! The man who carved this woodcut in 1702 lived in Sweden and had never even been to America.

Lenape families depended on animals for many things. For food, the Lenape fished and hunted deer and bears. The Lenape melted bear fat to make a lotion, which protected them from sunburn and insect bites in the summer and kept them warm in the winter. They fashioned animal bones and horns into tools. Even fish teeth, sharp and pointed, were sometimes used to tattoo Lenape people's bodies with images of animals.

In A.D. 1524, Lenape Indians living near the coast greeted Giovanni da Verrazano. Verrazano, an Italian navigator, explored the Atlantic coast and was the region's first European visitor. Almost 100 years passed before the Lenape saw another European.

In the early 1600s, Dutch navigator Henry Hudson explored the Atlantic coast and then sailed up what was later named the Hudson River before returning to the Netherlands. After Hudson's visit, the Dutch

Dutch explorer Henry Hudson navigated New Jersey's coast in 1609.

claimed much of the area that would become New Jersey, New York, Delaware, and Connecticut. They called the territory New Netherland.

The Dutch established trading posts along the Hudson and Delaware Rivers. There they gave brass kettles, guns, and blankets to Indians in exchange for furs. The Dutch made money selling these furs in Europe.

In 1629 the Dutch decided to set up a **colony,** or settlement, in North America. They started a system whereby a Dutchman could get a large piece of land in New Netherland if he agreed to take at least 50 people with him. Once in New Netherland, the landowner, called a **patroon,** was in charge of the people and the land.

Other Europeans were also attracted to New Netherland. Around 1640 the Swedes built two forts along the southern banks of the Delaware River. The Dutch, who wanted complete control in New Netherland, were not happy with the Swedish settlements. In 1655 Dutch soldiers took over the Swedish forts.

Philip Carteret *(center)* came to North America from Great Britain in 1665 to become New Jersey's governor. In this painting, he arrives at Newark Bay.

By this time, the British also had colonies in North America. King Charles II of Britain wanted to take over New Netherland to expand his North American empire. In 1664 the king gave the Dutch lands to his brother James, duke of York. James named part of the land New Jersey, after the British island of Jersey. The duke then sent soldiers to New Netherland to force out the Dutch, who proved to be much weaker than the British army.

In other British colonies, European settlers weren't always able to practice their religion freely. When settlers in nearby colonies heard that New Jersey would protect religious freedom, many of them moved to the colony. Baptists and Quakers settled in eastern New Jersey. In 1666 Puritans from Connecticut moved to New Jersey and founded the town of Newark.

As settlers came to New Jersey, they brought deadly diseases such as measles and smallpox. The Lenape had never before been exposed to these illnesses. Thousands of Indians died. Many others left New Jersey, heading west to what would later become Pennsylvania and Ohio. About 24,000 Lenape Indians probably lived in New Jersey before Europeans came. Only 3,000 were left in 1702.

Like many people in the colonies, New Jerseyans were unhappy under British rule. The British government forced colonists to pay high taxes on paper, glass, tea, and other goods that came from Great Britain. In 1774 a group of New Jerseyans in Greenwich protested against these taxes by burning a shipload of British tea. Less than a year after the Greenwich Tea Burning, New Jersey joined the other 12 British colonies in a war against Great Britain.

During the American Revolution, the British army wanted control of two of the richest and most important colonial cities—New York and Philadelphia. Because New Jersey lay in between, many battles, such as the Battle of Monmouth, were fought there.

After years of fighting, the British lost the war in 1783, and the United States was born. On December 18, 1787, New Jersey became the third state in the Union after adopting the U.S. Constitution, a written statement of the country's laws.

New Jerseyans worked hard to rebuild their state, much of which had been destroyed during the Revolutionary War. Transportation began to improve in the 1790s, when the state's first bridges were built. To cross rivers, travelers no longer had to rely on ferryboats, which were slow and unreliable.

Soon roads were improving, too. By 1829 New Jerseyans had built 51 **turnpikes,** or pay-as-you-go roads. A horse and rider, for example, had to pay one cent for every mile traveled—half a cent for the horse and half a cent for the rider.

Molly Pitcher

One of New Jersey's most famous women is Mary Hays—better known as Molly Pitcher. She played a small role in the American Revolution.

Molly's husband, John, fought in the Battle of Monmouth in June 1778. While John and other colonial soldiers were firing their cannons in the summer heat,

Molly carried buckets of water to them, thus earning her nickname, Molly Pitcher.

At one point, John was wounded and fell to the ground. Without hesitating, Molly took her husband's place and helped to fire the cannon. Years later, Molly was given $40 a year in recognition of her service to the colonial army.

With the construction of new railroads, people from New York City and Philadelphia could take short weekend trips to New Jersey's Atlantic shoreline.

In the 1830s, several railroad companies built tracks across northern New Jersey. The Camden and Atlantic Railroad made its first run across southern New Jersey in 1854, carrying passengers to a new resort, or vacation town, called Atlantic City.

As transportation continued to improve, New Jersey's industries grew rapidly. Trains brought iron ore from the state's northern hills to factories in Paterson and Trenton, where the iron was made into steel. The steel was then used to make locomotives and the cables for bridges.

Factory workers weave cloth. By 1860 New Jersey had become the sixth most important manufacturing state in the country.

Factories in Newark made just about everything—leather, clothing, carriages, knives, jewelry, tools, saddles, mirrors, and scissors. All of these goods, along with fruits and vegetables grown in southern New Jersey, were shipped to other states from the docks at Newark, Camden, and Jersey City.

Many of New Jersey's products were shipped to Southern states, where most people still made a living from farming. Many Southern farmers used slaves to do the work. But slavery was against the law in Northern states like New Jersey. Unable to settle their disagreements about slavery and other issues, the North and the South went to war in 1861.

Siding with the North, New Jersey sent 88,000 soldiers to serve in the Civil War. The state's industries boomed. Day and night, factories produced equipment for the war—locomotives, uniforms, blankets, tents, and rifles. New Jersey's railroads transported goods and troops to the South, where most of the battles were fought.

After the North won the war in 1865, railroad companies laid even more tracks across New Jersey.

A poster from the Civil War calls for recruits in Newark, New Jersey, to join the Northern army.

After arriving in the United States, many immigrants found jobs in New Jersey's factories. Many worked for 15 hours a day, 7 days a week, for very low pay.

Towns and factories sprang up wherever the railroads went, and by 1876 most people lived within six miles of a railway. In fact, many rich people began to buy homes in New Jersey, taking the train to their jobs in New York and Philadelphia.

In the 1880s, people from Italy, Poland, Hungary, Greece, and Russia began leaving their homelands in large numbers, hoping to find a better life in the United States. Thousands of these **immigrants** came to New Jersey. Many took factory jobs in the state's northern cities. Others went to the southern part of the state to farm. Still others found jobs mining iron ore in northwestern New Jersey.

In 1890 New Jersey had close to 1.5 million residents. Immigrants continued to come to the state, and by 1915 New Jersey was home to almost 3 million people.

Many of these people worked in New Jersey's factories, which produced much of the equipment needed during World War I (1914–1918). Workers made bullets, gunpowder, uniforms, airplanes, and ships. Soldiers from around the country trained at Fort Dix and Fort Merritt in New Jersey.

At Fort Dix, soldiers fill out paperwork. The camp was built in 1917 near Wrightstown, New Jersey, to train soldiers for World War I. The camp had 1,600 buildings and could house 70,000 people.

During World War II, many women in New Jersey went to work in factories.

New Jersey's industrial power was called upon again during World War II (1939–1945). Factory workers made uniforms, ammunition, airplane engines, and ships. Scientists in New Jersey did some research that led to the manufacture of the first atomic bomb.

After the war, New Jersey's population grew, and many families decided to leave the state's crowded cities. People built houses outside the cities, creating communities called suburbs. To get to work from the suburbs, many people drove on a new highway called the New Jersey Turnpike, which was completed in 1952.

As New Jerseyans settled in the suburbs, they spent less and less of their money in the state's cities. Suburban residents, who were mainly white people, also paid taxes to their local suburban governments instead of to those of the cities. Cities had less money to support schools and to repair roads. As a result, New Jersey's cities began to decay. Many businesses closed, and houses and buildings started to fall apart.

Many black New Jerseyans, who could not afford to move to the suburbs, were angry about living conditions in the state's crumbling cities. Riots broke out in the black neighborhoods of several of these cities during the summer of 1967. More than two dozen people were killed in Newark, where the worst rioting took place.

New Jersey's government realized that something had to change. But to improve living conditions, the state needed money. So in the late 1960s, New Jersey set up a **lottery**, a state-run game in which people buy tickets to win prizes. The state also added a tax to items sold in stores. And in 1976, New Jersey's voters agreed to allow **gambling,** or betting on games, to take place in Atlantic City. The state uses the money it earns from these sources to build schools, office buildings, neighborhood centers, and highways.

Not all of New Jersey's problems have been solved, though. Many New Jerseyans are still very poor. And with so many people and industries, pollution is a big problem.

New Jersey tried to improve living conditions in cities in the 1960s and 1970s by building giant housing projects like this one in Newark.

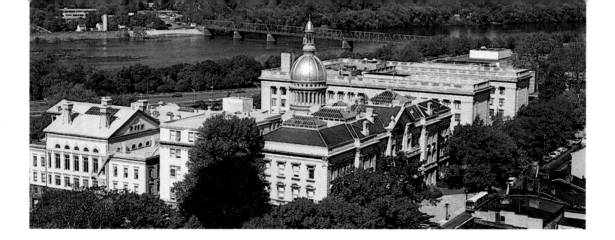

New Jersey's capitol building in Trenton

New Jerseyans elected the state's first female governor, Christine Todd Whitman, in 1993. Whitman served in that post until 2001, when President George W. Bush appointed her administrator of the Environmental Protection Agency. During Whitman's time as governor, the crime rate in the state fell. Hundreds of thousands of new jobs were created. New Jerseyans began working to expand high-tech industries in their state. And they started cleaning up their state's air and waterways. Polluted former industrial sites were also being cleaned up so that they could be used for new businesses. Working together, New Jerseyans can continue to set examples for solving problems.

PEOPLE & ECONOMY

Farms, Factories, and Fun

If you've ever played the game Monopoly, you already know something about the state of New Jersey. Monopoly is a game about buying and selling property in Atlantic City—one of New Jersey's most famous resort towns. More than 30 million people visit Atlantic City each year. That's more than four times the number of people who live in the entire state!

With 8.4 million residents, New Jersey is one of the most populated states in the country. And because it is small, New Jersey is the most crowded state. On average, for every square mile in New Jersey, you will find more than 1,000 people.

A crowded neighborhood in South Seaside Park, New Jersey

Atlantic City is New Jersey's busiest tourist attraction.

Most New Jerseyans—about 89 percent—live in urban areas, or cities. Only California has a higher percentage of city dwellers. New Jersey's largest cities are Newark, Jersey City, Paterson, Elizabeth, and Edison. Trenton is the state capital.

White people make up about 66 percent of New Jersey's population. About 13 percent of New Jerseyans are African Americans. The number of Latinos living in New Jersey grew by about 50 percent during the 1990s. Latinos now make up about 13 percent of the state's population. Nearly 6 percent of New Jerseyans are Asian American. A very small number of Native Americans live in New Jersey.

New Jerseyans watch a street parade.

New Jersey is known as the Garden State because of the many flowers, fruits, and vegetables grown here.

Before factories were built in New Jersey, most people made a living from farming. In modern New Jersey, only 1 percent of the state's workers have jobs in agriculture. Gardeners in New Jersey's greenhouses grow millions of roses each year, as well as chrysanthemums, geraniums, and lilies.

Throughout New Jersey, farmers grow fruits and vegetables such as tomatoes, cabbages, lettuce, potatoes, and sweet corn. Blueberries and cran-berries are important crops from the Pinelands. Farmers raise dairy cattle in northwestern New Jersey.

Many New Jerseyans, such as this worker in a soap factory, have jobs in industry.

About 11 percent of New Jersey's workers have jobs in manufacturing. Many of New Jersey's factories are in big cities such as Newark and Jersey City. The state leads the nation in its output of chemicals. Some of the chemical products made in New Jersey are medicine, shampoo, laundry detergent, and paint.

Food-processing plants in southwestern New Jersey package fruits and vegetables grown by the state's farmers. Other factories make computers, clothing, and medical instruments. The telephone in your house was probably made in New Jersey, too!

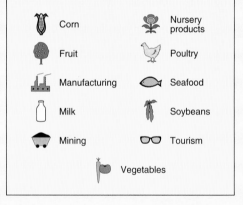

NEW JERSEY
Economic Map

The symbols on this map show where different economic activities take place in New Jersey. The legend below explains what each symbol stands for.

Corn		Nursery products	
Fruit		Poultry	
Manufacturing		Seafood	
Milk		Soybeans	
Mining		Tourism	
	Vegetables		

Some New Jerseyans make a living from fishing. New Jersey's fishing industry earns the state about $100 million each year.

Most of New Jersey's workers—about 71 percent—have service jobs. Instead of making products, service workers help people. New Jersey's service workers include salesclerks, waiters, doctors, and agents who sell homes and office buildings. The researchers who work in New Jersey's many laboratories have service jobs, too. Thirteen percent of New Jerseyans work for the state or federal government.

New Jerseyans have little trouble finding places to enjoy themselves. Along the state's coast, people swim, surf, and hunt for seashells. Boating is popular, too. Small boats take advantage of a sheltered water route called the Atlantic Intracoastal Waterway. Running along the Atlantic coast from Massachusetts to Florida, this waterway is protected from the rest of the ocean by a string of islands and sandbars.

Visitors to Atlantic City often enjoy a stroll along the Boardwalk.

Atlantic City, one of the largest seaside resorts in the world, lies on New Jersey's southern coast. Stretching along the ocean, the city's famous wooden sidewalk—the Boardwalk—is lined with **casinos,** or gambling houses, hotels, restaurants, and shops. One of the best-known spots on the Boardwalk is the Convention Center, where the Miss America Pageant is held each September.

New Jersey's Atlantic coast is a popular place for boating *(left)*. A boy builds a sand castle *(above)* along the Atlantic Ocean near Cape May, New Jersey.

Many New Jerseyans enjoy watching horse races at Monmouth Park.

The New Jersey Devils are one of several teams that New Jerseyans cheer on in the state's Meadowlands Sports Complex.

Sports fans go wild in New Jersey. Two professional football teams—the New York Giants and the New York Jets—play in the huge Meadowlands Sports Complex in East Rutherford, New Jersey. The New Jersey Nets swish the hoops on the complex's basketball court, while the New Jersey Devils pass the puck in the Meadowlands's hockey arena.

People looking for a quieter place can visit Princeton University. Founded in 1746, Princeton is the fourth oldest university in the United States. Among the school's many historical buildings is Nassau Hall, which was the site of the U.S. Capitol in 1783.

New York City's skyline can be seen from Jersey City, New Jersey.

History buffs touring the Hancock House in south-western New Jersey see how early Quaker colonists lived. Walking in Monmouth Battlefield State Park, visitors can try to imagine the Revolutionary War battle that took place at this site more than 200 years ago. In West Orange, faces light up at the Edison National Historic Site. Here in his laboratory and workshops, Thomas Edison invented the movie camera and the record player.

People are sometimes surprised to discover that New Jersey, which is crisscrossed by highways, has more than 50 state parks and forests. Walking along the trails that pass through High Point State Park, hikers might spot a bear or a bobcat. Visitors to Liberty State Park near Jersey City can look across the New York Bay to see New York City's skyline and the Statue of Liberty.

Hikers following the Batona Trail through New Jersey's Pinelands will walk through three state forests before completing the 48-mile wilderness route. And along the way, a visitor just might see the Jersey Devil—a legendary creature said to have the body of a kangaroo, the head of a dog, the face of a horse, the wings of a bat, the feet of a pig, and a forked tail!

Bobcats roam High Point State Park.

THE ENVIRONMENT

Protecting the Pinelands

ith a population of 8.4 million people, New Jersey is a crowded place. Houses, shopping malls, restaurants, hotels, factories, offices, trains, cars, and buses meet the eye in all directions. As the population continues to grow, developers put up more houses and build more resorts and roads.

But overdevelopment happens when people build too much, causing problems in the environment. When trees are cut down to make way for new buildings and roads, animals lose a place to live and raise their young. New roads also bring in more automobiles, trucks, and buses, which pollute the air with their exhaust.

Much of New Jersey's forestland has been destroyed to make space for roads and highways.

In the 1970s, New Jerseyans decided to do something about overdevelopment in their state. They decided to preserve more than 1 million acres of land known as the Pinelands (or the Pine Barrens)

in southern New Jersey. From the story of the Pinelands, New Jerseyans know that they can work together to protect their environment.

The Pinelands is an area of cedar swamps, forests of dwarf oak and pine trees, twisting rivers, and insect-eating plants such as the northern pitcher and the sundew. Animals such as the Pine Barrens tree frog and the bog turtle, which are in danger of becoming extinct, live in the Pinelands. In the central part of the Pinelands, cranberry and blueberry farmers harvest their crops. Small towns and historic villages dot the landscape.

Ever since white settlers first came to New Jersey, people have been trying to develop the Pinelands. At different times throughout the history of the Pinelands, people have come to farm, to cut down trees, to mine iron, and to tap water from the Cohansey Aquifer—a giant underground storehouse of fresh water.

Pine Barrens tree frog

Winding rivers in the Pinelands are great for canoeing.

One of the most serious threats to the Pinelands was the growth of nearby Atlantic City in the 1970s. After gambling was legalized in 1976, people rushed to the city to build hotels, restaurants, and casinos. New Jerseyans worried that Atlantic City would grow bigger and expand into the Pinelands, spoiling the land and polluting—or even using up—the water in the Cohansey Aquifer.

In 1977 a group of New Jerseyans formed the Pine Barrens Coalition to speak out against overdevelopment in the Pinelands. In 1978 New Jersey's government responded by passing laws to protect the water of the Cohansey Aquifer. That same year, the U.S. Congress established the Pinelands National Reserve—the first reserve in the United States. This means that government groups, such as the Pinelands Commission, work to protect the land, animals, plants, and waters from the dangers of overdevelopment. And in 1983, the United Nations designated the area as one of only a few international reserves.

The Pinelands were once threatened by the urban sprawl of Atlantic City. But many New Jerseyans worked hard to protect the Pinelands.

Some people are unhappy with the government's rules to limit development in the Pinelands. Residents feel that they no longer have control of their land. Others fear that the Pinelands aren't being protected enough. They say that the government has not been as dedicated to preserving the Pinelands as it once was. For example, the government approved some new development in the Pinelands in the late 1990s, such as a new school and the expansion of commercial cranberry bogs.

The New Jersey government continues to balance the needs of the local residents and the need to protect New Jersey's natural treasure. Located in the most populated region of the country, the Pinelands stands as the largest wilderness area between Boston and Washington, D.C. New Jerseyans are striving to keep it that way.

Blueberries grow in the Pinelands.

Fun Facts

The first drive-in movie theater opened in 1933 outside Camden, New Jersey. The theater had parking spaces for 500 cars and showed two films a night.

The first dinosaur skeleton ever discovered in North America was found in Haddonfield, New Jersey, in 1858. The fossil was a hadrosaur—a 30-foot dinosaur that had webbed toes, hundreds of teeth, and a beak like a duck's.

The electric light bulb was invented by Thomas Edison at his laboratory in Menlo Park, New Jersey, in 1879.

Thomas Edison also invented the movie camera in New Jersey. For awhile, the state was the filmmaking center of the world. During the early 1900s, hundreds of films were made in Fort Lee, New Jersey, before the industry moved west to California.

New Jersey is important in sports history. The first organized baseball game was played in Hoboken in 1846. The first college football game was played in New Brunswick in 1869—Rutgers University beat Princeton University. And the first professional basketball game was played in Trenton in 1896.

In 1877 the first interstate long-distance telephone call took place between New Brunswick, New Jersey, and New York, New York.

Many people call Atlantic City the Saltwater Taffy Capital of the World. The candy became known as saltwater taffy after seawater drenched a taffy-vendor's stand in Atlantic City in the 1880s.

STATE SONG

New Jersey has no official state song. But New Jerseyans wishing to celebrate the beauty of their state can sing "Ode to New Jersey." The song borrows the melody of the German Christmas carol "O Tannenbaum," as do state songs from Michigan, Maryland, and Iowa.

ODE TO NEW JERSEY

Words and music traditional

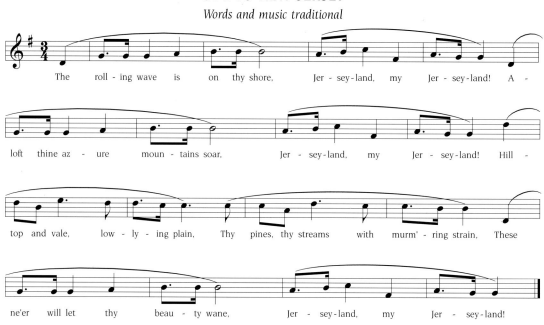

The roll-ing wave is on thy shore, Jer-sey-land, my Jer-sey-land! A-

loft thine az - ure moun-tains soar, Jer - sey-land, my Jer - sey-land! Hill -

top and vale, low - ly - ing plain, Thy pines, thy streams with murm' - ring strain, These

ne'er will let thy beau - ty wane, Jer - sey-land, my Jer - sey-land!

A NEW JERSEY RECIPE

At the New Jersey shore, saltwater taffy comes in
many flavors, from chocolate to cherry. You can make
it almost any flavor you want. Try peppermint, orange, vanilla, or almond. All of
these flavors are available in the grocery store as extracts. For a batch this size, use
about 1 teaspoon of extract and three drops of food coloring.

NEW JERSEY SHORE SALTWATER TAFFY

1 cup sugar
1 tablespoon cornstarch
⅔ cup light corn syrup
1 tablespoon butter

½ cup water
¼ teaspoon salt
food coloring and flavoring

1. Mix sugar and cornstarch in saucepan.
2. Stir in corn syrup, butter, water, salt.
3. Cook mixture over medium heat until it reaches 254° F on a candy thermometer
   or until a few drops in cold water form hard balls.
4. Remove pan from heat and stir in a few drops of food coloring and flavoring of
   your choice (see note above).
5. Pour taffy onto buttered baking sheet.
6. Cool taffy for two or three minutes, until you can handle it comfortably. If it gets
   too cool, you can warm it in a 350° F oven for three to four minutes.
7. Divide taffy into two or three balls.
8. Butter your hands, and pull lump of taffy until it is about 15 inches long. Double it
   up and pull again. Repeat until it is light in color and firm enough to hold a shape.
9. Stretch it into a rope about ¾ inch in diameter and snip off 1-inch bits with oiled
   kitchen scissors. Wrap each piece in wax paper.

HISTORICAL TIMELINE

10,000 B.C.   Ancestors of the Lenape arrive in the New Jersey area.

A.D. 1500   The Lenape settle along New Jersey's Atlantic coast.

1524   Giovanni da Verrazano explores the Atlantic coast.

1609   Henry Hudson sails up the Hudson River.

1629   The Dutch set up a North American colony in New Netherland.

1664   The British army forces Dutch colonists out of New Netherland.

1666   Puritans from Connecticut settle the town of Newark.

1774   New Jerseyans protest against high taxes at the Greenwich Tea Burning.

1776   The Revolutionary War (1776–1783) begins.

1787   New Jersey becomes the third state.

1829   New Jersey has 51 turnpikes.

1854 Train service to Atlantic City begins.

1861 The Civil War (1861–1865) begins, and New Jersey sides with the North.

1890 New Jersey has 1.5 million residents.

1915 Immigration swells New Jersey's population to 3 million.

1952 The New Jersey Turnpike is completed.

1967 Twenty-six people die in Newark during race riots.

1976 Gambling is allowed in Atlantic City.

1983 The Pinelands, a national park, becomes an international reserve.

1993 Christine Todd Whitman was elected New Jersey's first woman governor.

2001 Christine Todd Whitman leaves her position as governor to be the administrator of the Environmental Protection Agency.

John Amos

Judy Blume

Stephen Crane

OUTSTANDING NEW JERSEYANS

John Amos (born 1942) is an actor from Newark. Amos played the part of Kunte Kinte in the TV mini-series *Roots* and starred as James Evans in the television series *Good Times*. He has also appeared in many motion pictures, including *Die Hard 2*.

Judy Blume (born 1938) of Elizabeth, New Jersey, writes books for adults and young people. Her titles include *Tales of a Fourth Grade Nothing, Blubber,* and *Tiger Eyes*. Many people like Blume's books because they use everyday language to tell about real-life situations.

Edna Woolman Chase (1877–1957) was the editor-in-chief of *Vogue* magazine from 1914 to 1955. In 1944 she organized the first fashion show in the United States. Chase was born in Asbury Park, New Jersey.

James Fenimore Cooper (1789–1851) is best known for a series of novels called *The Leather-Stocking Tales*. In writing these books, he became the first author to realistically describe life on the American frontier. Cooper was born in Burlington, New Jersey.

Stephen Crane (1871–1900) was born in Newark and became one of the most famous writers of his time. His book *The Red Badge of Courage*, which is set during the Civil War, tells of the horrors of war.

Mary Elizabeth Mapes Dodge (1831–1905) began her writing career after moving to Newark at the age of 27. Dodge is best known for her children's book *Hans Brinker, or, The Silver Skates*, which tells the story of a young Dutch boy who competes in an ice-skating race.

Mary Elizabeth Mapes Dodge

William Pène Du Bois (1916–1993) was a children's writer and illustrator. Born in Nutley, New Jersey, Du Bois won the Newbery Medal in 1948 for his book *The Twenty-One Balloons.*

Franco Harris (born 1950) played football with the Pittsburgh Steelers for 12 years. Harris helped his team win four Super Bowls, and he ran more than 1,000 yards each season for eight years. The quick running back was born in Fort Dix, New Jersey.

Franco Harris

Charles E. Hires (1851–1937) introduced his new soft drink, root beer, at the 1876 Centennial Exposition in Philadelphia, Pennsylvania. The inventor, born near Roadstown, New Jersey, patented his formula and began to sell the popular Hires Root Beer.

Charles E. Hires

Whitney Houston (born 1963) has a voice that caught many people's attention when she was still in grade school. Her first album, released in 1985, sold over 14 million copies worldwide. Since then she has won Grammy Awards for "I Wanna Dance with Somebody," "I Will Always Love You," and "It's Not Right but It's Okay." Houston was born in Newark.

Whitney Houston

Dorothea Lange (1895–1965), from Hoboken, is famous for the photographs she took of families during the Great Depression. These pictures, published in newspapers and magazines, convinced people to support programs that would help needy families. Lange traveled all over the world during her career, taking pictures in Asia, Africa, and South America.

Dorothea Lange

Jacob Lawrence (1917–2000) was a painter from Atlantic City. Some of his paintings, such as *The Life of Harriet Tubman*, are collections of 40 or more panels that illustrate African American history.

Joe Medwick

Jack Nicholson

Alice Paul

Paul Simon

Jerry Lewis (born 1926) was born in Newark as Jerome Levitch. The comedian teamed up with performer Dean Martin to make a string of successful movies. Lewis went on to star in television and more movies, including the original version of *The Nutty Professor*.

Joe Medwick (1911–1975) played baseball with the St. Louis Cardinals. In 1937 he won baseball's Triple Crown by leading the National League in home runs, runs batted in, and batting average. Medwick was born in Carteret, New Jersey.

Jack Nicholson (born 1937) is a well-known actor who has starred in many movies. He won Academy Awards for his performances in *One Flew Over the Cuckoo's Nest* and *Terms of Endearment* as well as Golden Globe Awards for his roles in *Prizzi's Honor* and *As Good as It Gets*. Nicholson is from Neptune, New Jersey.

Alice Paul (1885–1977), born in Moorestown, New Jersey, was a leader in the fight for equal rights for women. Paul founded the National Woman's Party in 1913 and worked for women's right to vote, which was granted in 1920.

Zebulon Pike (1779–1813) was an explorer. As an officer in the U.S. Army, he searched for the source of the Mississippi River and scouted the southwest United States. Pikes Peak in Colorado is named for the native of Lamberton.

Paul Simon (born 1941) is a famous singer and songwriter. While in his teens, he met Art Garfunkel, with whom he performed for many years, creating hit songs like "Mrs. Robinson" and "Bridge over Troubled Water." In 1971 Simon began to perform on his own. His solo album *Graceland* won a Grammy Award in 1987. Simon was born in Newark.

Frank Sinatra (1915–1998) was a popular singer for over 50 years. Sinatra also acted in more than 60 films, winning an Academy Award in 1953 for his role in *From Here to Eternity*. Sinatra was born in Hoboken.

Frank Sinatra

Kevin Spacey (born 1959) is an actor known for his performances in motion pictures and on stage. He won Academy Awards for his roles in *The Usual Suspects* and *American Beauty*. Spacey is from South Orange, New Jersey.

Kevin Spacey

Bruce Springsteen (born 1949) is a popular singer and songwriter. In 1973 he started the E Street Band. With albums such as *Born to Run* and *Born in the U.S.A.*, Springsteen became one of the most popular rock stars of his time. Springsteen was born in Freehold, New Jersey.

Bruce Springsteen

Alfred Stieglitz (1864–1946), born in Hoboken, was a photographer who helped establish photography as an art form. In 1903 Stieglitz started a magazine called *Camera Work*. Two years later, he started an art gallery in New York City, where he showed paintings, sculptures, and photographs done by promising American and European artists.

Meryl Streep (born 1949) of Summit, New Jersey, has appeared in many motion pictures, on stage, and in television films. She won Academy Awards for her performances in *Kramer vs. Kramer* and *Sophie's Choice*.

Meryl Streep

Woodrow Wilson (1856–1924) moved to New Jersey in 1890 to teach at Princeton University, later becoming the university's president. After serving as governor of New Jersey, he went on to become the 28th president of the United States.

FACTS-AT-A-GLANCE

Nickname: Garden State

Song: no official state song

Motto: Liberty and Prosperity

Flower: purple violet

Tree: red oak

Bird: eastern goldfinch

Animal: horse

Fish: brook trout

Shell: knobbed whelk

Fossil: Hadrosaurus *foulkii*

Date and ranking of statehood:
   December 18, 1787, the 3rd state

Capital: Trenton

Area: 7,419 square miles

Rank in area, nationwide: 46th

Average January temperature: 31° F

Average July temperature: 75° F

Two female figures support a blue shield in the center of New Jersey's flag. The woman on the left carries a pole topped with a liberty cap—a symbol of freedom. The woman on the right holds a horn filled with fruits and vegetables, which stands for agricultural wealth.

POPULATION GROWTH

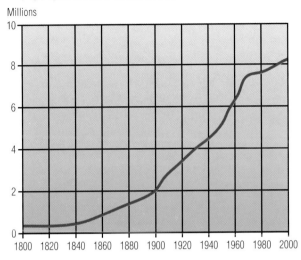

Millions

This chart shows how New Jersey's population has grown from 1800 to 2000.

New Jersey's state seal was adopted in 1928. It is very similar to the state's flag.

Population: 8,414,350 (2000 census)

Rank in population, nationwide: 9th

Major cities and populations: (2000 census) Newark (273,546), Jersey City (240,055), Paterson (149,222), Elizabeth (120,568), Edison (97,687)

U.S. senators: 2

U.S. representatives: 13

Electoral votes: 15

Natural resources: clay, granite, greensand marl, peat, sand and gravel, soil, zinc

Agricultural products: blueberries, cabbages, corn, cranberries, eggs, milk, nursery products, peaches, potatoes, soybeans, tomatoes

Fishing industry: clams, flounder, lobsters, menhaden, oysters, scallops, sea bass, whiting

Manufactured goods: chemical products, detergents, electrical equipment, food products, medicines, paints, printed materials, shampoos

WHERE NEW JERSEYANS WORK

Services—71 percent (services includes jobs in trade; community, social, and personal services; finance, insurance, and real estate; transportation, communication, and utilities)

Government—13 percent

Manufacturing—11 percent

Construction—4 percent

Agriculture—1 percent

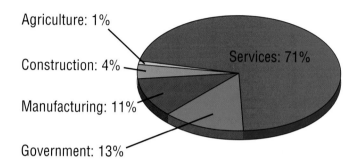

Agriculture: 1%
Construction: 4%
Manufacturing: 11%
Government: 13%
Services: 71%

GROSS STATE PRODUCT

Services—72 percent

Manufacturing—13 percent

Government—11 percent

Construction—3 percent

Agriculture—1 percent

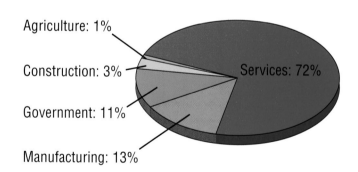

Agriculture: 1%
Construction: 3%
Government: 11%
Manufacturing: 13%
Services: 72%

NEW JERSEY WILDLIFE

Mammals: deer, fox, mink, muskrat, opossum, otter, rabbit, raccoon, skunk

Birds: duck, goose, grouse, partridge, pheasant, quail, wild turkey

Fish: bass, bluefish, clam, crab, crappie, lobster, pickerel, oyster, pike, salmon, shad, sturgeon, trout

Reptiles and amphibians: eastern box turtle, eastern diamondback rattlesnake, eastern spadefoot, fowler's toad, green frog, northern fence lizard

Trees: beech, birch, cedar, maple, oak, pine, yellow poplar

Wild plants: azalea, buttercup, goldenrod, honeysuckle, mountain laurel, purple violet, Queen Anne's lace, rhododendron

Eastern box turtle

PLACES TO VISIT

Barnegat Lighthouse, Long Beach Island
Each year thousand of visitors climb to the top of this scenic lighthouse, which dates back to 1835. From the observation deck you can view Long Beach Island and Island Beach State Park. And on clear summer nights, the observation deck is open for star gazing.

Batsto Historic Village, Hammonton
Visitors can see more than two centuries of history at this well-preserved historic village. From the 1760s until the end of the Civil War, Batsto was known for its iron and glass industries. It was later remade to reflect the style of the late 1800s.

Delaware Water Gap, New Jersey-Pennsylvania border
With cliffs on both sides, this natural gorge runs between New Jersey and Pennsylvania. Carved by the Delaware River, the gorge is part of the larger Delaware Water Gap National Recreation Center.

Discovery Seashell Museum, Ocean City
Do you love to collect seashells? This unusual museum displays and sells seashells and corals from around the world.

Barnegat Lighthouse

Double Trouble State Park, Berkeley

This state park was a lumber operation and a cranberry farm during the 1800s. The park features nature trails, cranberry bogs, and the historic Double Trouble village.

Edison National Historic Site, West Orange

In 1887 inventor Thomas Edison opened a large laboratory in West Orange. Over the next 44 years, Edison invented more than half of his 1,093 patents in this laboratory. Visitors can view the chemistry laboratory, machine shop, the library where Edison did his research, and Edison's home.

Liberty Science Center, Jersey City

Located in Jersey City's Liberty Park, the Liberty Science Center houses an IMAX theater and hundreds of hands-on exhibits covering a wide range of science topics.

Newark Museum Complex, Newark

The largest museum complex in New Jersey features an art museum, a planetarium, a small zoo, gift shops, a cafe, an auditorium, and a sculpture garden.

New Jersey State Aquarium, Camden

This aquarium features a 760,000-gallon fish tank that holds about 40 different species of fish. The aquarium also features interactive exhibits about ocean life.

Six Flags Great Adventure amusement park, Jackson

If you like fast, scary, or wet rides, then spend a day at this large theme park. The park features more than 100 rides and attractions, including a drive-through animal safari.

ANNUAL EVENTS

Super Science Weekend, Trenton—*January*

Sail Expo, Atlantic City—*February and March*

Cherry Blossom Display, Newark—*April*

National Marbles Tournament, Wildwood—*June*

New Jersey Festival of Ballooning, Readington—*July*

Whitesbog Blueberry Festival, Browns Mills—*July*

Barnegat Bay Crab Race and Seafood Festival,
    Seaside Heights—*August*

Cranberry Festival, Chatsworth—*October*

Reenactment of George Washington's Crossing of the Delaware,
    Washington Crossing—*December*

LEARN MORE ABOUT NEW JERSEY

BOOKS

General

Fradin, Dennis Brindell. *New Jersey.* Chicago: Children's Press, 1993.

Stein, R. Conrad. *New Jersey.* New York: Children's Press, 1998.
  For older readers.

Topper, Frank, and Charles A. Wills. *A Historical Album of New Jersey.* Brookfield, CT: Millbrook Press, 1995.

Special Interest

Beirne, Barbara. *Siobhan's Journey: A Belfast Girl Visits the United States.* Minneapolis: Carolrhoda Books, Inc., 1993. Ten-year-old Siobhan McNulty has traveled from Belfast, Northern Ireland, to spend six weeks with a family in New Jersey. Colorful photographs complement this first-person account of the differences between Northern Ireland and the United States.

Hansen, Judith. *Seashells in My Pocket: A Child's Nature Guide to Exploring the Atlantic.* Boston: Appalachian Mountain Club Books, 1992. An introduction to the plants and animals that live along the Atlantic shore from Maine to North Carolina.

Harris, Jack. *New Jersey Nets.* Mankato, MN: The Creative Co., 1997. Learn about the history of New Jersey's basketball team, from its beginnings in 1967.

Mitchell, Barbara. *The Wizard of Sound: A Story about Thomas Edison.* Minneapolis: Carolrhoda Books, Inc., 1991. This biography follows the famous inventor's life, from his sickly childhood in the Midwest to the building of his laboratory in Menlo Park, New Jersey, where he created his favorite invention, the phonograph.

Fiction

Avi. *Captain Grey.* New York: Morrow Jr. Books, 1993. After the Revolutionary War, an 11-year-old boy begins a dangerous adventure when he is kidnapped off the New Jersey Coast by a ruthless pirate named Captain Grey.

Cuyler, Margery. *The Battlefield Ghost.* New York: Scholastic, 1999. John and his sister Lisa have been hearing rumors that their new house in Princeton, New Jersey, is haunted by the ghost of a soldier from the Revolutionary War. When strange things happen in the house, John and Lisa begin to suspect that the rumors may be true.

Karr, Kathleen. *Man of the Family.* New York: Farrar, Straus & Giroux, 1999. In this engaging historical novel, 10-year-old Istvan tells the story of his immigrant family's struggle to adjust from life in Hungary to life on their farm in South Jersey in the 1920s.

Knight, James E. *The Village: Life in Colonial Times.* Mahwah, NJ: Troll Communications, 1997. Take a journey back in time with author James Knight as he describes the lives and work of New Jerseyans in an early 1700s farming village.

Myers, Walter Dean. *Me, Mop, and the Moondance Kid.* New York: Delacorte Press, 1988. This Newbery Honor–winning author has written a warm-hearted, funny book about the ups and downs of three orphans—T. J., Mop, and Moondance—who live in New Jersey.

WEBSITES

State of New Jersey
<http://www.state.nj.us/>
New Jersey's official website includes information about the state's government, economy, transportation, and education.

Official New Jersey Travel and Tourism Website
<http://www.state.nj.us/travel/index.html>
This website features general information about activities and attractions throughout New Jersey and travel information about specific cities.

The *Star-Ledger*
< http://www.nj.com/news/ledger/>
Read about current events in the online version of this popular New Jersey newspaper, based in Newark.

New Jersey Facts and Symbols
<http://www.state.nj.us/njfacts/njfacts.htm>
For answers to your questions about the Garden State, visit this fact-packed website.

PRONUNCIATION GUIDE

Appalachian (ap-uh-LAY-chuhn)

Cohansey Aquifer (koh-HAN-see AK-wuh-fur)

Hopatcong (huh-PAT-kahn)

Kittatinny (KIHT-uh-TIHN-ee)

Lenape (luh-NAH-pay)

Monmouth (MAHN-muth)

Newark (NOO-urk)

Passaic (puh-SAY-ihk)

Paterson (PAT-ur-suhn)

Piedmont (PEED-mahnt)

Verrazano, Giovanni da (vehr-raht-SAHN-oh, joh-VAHN-nee dah)

GLOSSARY

casino: a room or building where people gamble

colony: a territory ruled by a country some distance away

Fall Line: A line that follows the points at which high, rocky land drops to low, sandy soil. Numerous waterfalls are created along this line when rivers tumble from the upland to the lowland. In the United States, a fall line runs from New Jersey to Alabama.

gambling: placing bets (usually money) on a game such as poker or dice

immigrant: a person who moves into a foreign country and settles there

lottery: A game of chance in which people pick numbers that they hope will match numbers chosen in a regularly scheduled drawing. Players pay a small fee for each numbered ticket. Winners cash in their tickets, sometimes for large sums of money.

patroon: a man who was given land in New Netherland that he could rent to others

plateau: a large, relatively flat area that stands above the surrounding land

precipitation: rain, snow, and other forms of moisture that fall to earth

turnpike: a highway on which a toll, or fee, is collected from drivers at various points along the route

INDEX

PHOTO ACKNOWLEDGMENTS

Cover photographs by © Kelly-Mooney Photography/Corbis (left) and © Kit Kittle/Corbis (right). Digital Cartographics, pp. 1, 8, 9, 44; © Jonathon Blair/Corbis, pp. 2–3; © Joe McDonald/Corbis, pp. 3, 73; © William W. Hawkins, pp. 4 (detail), 7 (detail), 17 (detail), 39 (detail), 42 (detail), 52 (detail), 55, 56; © Michael J. Kilpatrick, pp. 6, 7, 10, 16 (right), 45, 51, 53, 58, 59; © Tony LaGruth, pp. 11, 17, 50, 80; © Alan L. Detrick, pp. 12, 47 (left), 52, 57; © Nancy L. Erickson/New Wave Photography, pp. 13, 40, 46; © Saul Mayer, p. 14; © James Mejuto Photo, pp. 15, 47 (right), 48; © Clay Myers, p. 16 (left); John T. Kraft, Seton Hall University Museum, p. 19; The Library Company of Philadelphia, p. 20; Library of Congress, pp. 21, 22, 29; Special Collections and Archives, Rutgers University Libraries, pp. 24, 33; National Archives, pp. 27, 34; Newark Public Library, pp. 28, 31, 37, 68 (second from bottom), 66 (bottom); Bettman/Corbis, p. 32; © Joseph Moore, p. 38; © Bob Krist/Corbis, p. 39; © Jeff Greenberg, pp. 41, 43; © ALLSPORT USA/Jamie Squire, p. 49; © Betty Groskin, p. 54; Camden County Historical Society, N.J., p. 60; Toby Schnobrich, p. 61; Tim Seeley, pp. 63, 71, 72; Hollywood Book & Poster, pp. 66 (top), 68 (second from top and bottom), 69 (second from bottom and bottom); UPI/Bettmann/Corbis, p. 66 (second from top); *Dictionary of American Portraits*, p. 66 (second from bottom); Pittsburgh Steelers, p. 67 (top); The Procter & Gamble Company, p. 67 (second from top); Photofest, pp. 67 (second from bottom), 69 (second from top); Oakland Museum–Dorthea Lange Collection, p. 67 (bottom); Cleveland Public Library, p. 68 (top); Independent Picture Service, p. 69 (top); Jean Matheny, p. 70 (top); © Kelly-Mooney Photography/Corbis, p. 74.